A LITTLE

MISSIC_____

REMINDERS

BY MARK W. NEWMAN

COVENANT COMMUNICATIONS, INC.

Published by Covenant Communications, Inc.
American Fork, Utah

10 09 08   14 13 12 11

INTRODUCTION

After serving my mission in scenic southern Africa, I was called to be mission leader of my ward at Brigham Young University. Since I was living in the dorms, the ward consisted mostly of freshmen planning to serve missions at the end of the school year. My chief function was to teach the missionary preparation class.

During my two years in Africa, I had vowed that if I ever had the opportunity to work with prospective missionaries, I would let them know what it was *really* like out in the mission field. Sure, I wanted my class members to know about the thrill associated with finding that "golden" family. But I also wanted them to know about some of the other adventures – challenges like serving with a companion who doesn't follow every rule, having three bikes stolen in your zone within 72 hours, and not being transferred for over eight months.

I wanted my class members to write to me during their missions, so at the end of the school year I typed up a short note of thanks to them and included my home address. As an afterthought, I decided to add a few short pieces of advice, many of which had surfaced during the class. When I ran out of room on the page, I had recorded 65 reminders.

After that, the other 357 reminders came quickly. Some were contributed by friends, family members, and fellow returned missionaries.

I hope these reminders will help missionaries to be more successful in their efforts, while at the same time helping them to recognize the inherent humor in parts of the mission experience. After all, why wait to look back on it and laugh?

Whether you serve in Africa, Europe, or the States, I'm sure you'll relate to many of these reminders. The cultures may differ, but the gospel and its messengers are universal. Have a great mission!

DEDICATION

To Tim and Peggy Newman, the mission couple who converted me to the gospel through their stellar example, and to all of the unique missionaries who served in the South Africa, Cape Town mission between 1989 and 1991.

1 • Your mission call is between you and the Lord. So open it alone – away from family and friends.

2 • Start your mission journal a couple of weeks before you leave on your mission. Include entries about your farewell and feelings about saying goodbye to family and friends.

3 • Before entering the mission field, ask friends and family members to write brief notes in your journal. Don't read them until your first tough day.

4 • Memorize D&C 4 before entering the MTC.

5 • Renew your driver's license before leaving on your mission.

6 • After opening your call, write a brief letter to yourself and seal it. Three months into your mission, read the letter to remind you of your eagerness to serve.

7 • Take copies of your mission call, patriarchal blessing, and priesthood line of authority with you.

8 • Pray for confirmation that your mission call was issued through inspiration.

9 · The bishop has final responsibility for speaking assignments in all sacrament meetings, including your farewell and homecoming.

10 · You don't have to have your whole family speak at your farewell.

11 · Stay within designated time limits during your farewell and homecoming talks.

12 ♦ Buy socks of the same color so that when you get a hole in some, you'll still be able to make matches.

13 ♦ Practice your mom's ten best recipes *before* leaving on your mission.

14 ♦ It is inappropriate for the person giving the closing prayer at your farewell to ask for a blessing upon your open house refreshments.

15 • If you wear glasses, make sure you bring an extra pair. Bring along your prescription, too.

16 • No matter what the salesman tells you, no one actually uses cedar shoe stretchers in the mission field.

17 • Take full advantage of the "Speak Your Language" program in the MTC.

18 • Companions are Siamese twins joined at the Spirit.

19 • MTC food may not be Mom's cooking, but it's better than what you'll be eating in the coming weeks and months.

20 • Safeguard your passport and other important documents.

21 • If you play the piano, take a hymn book and some appropriate prelude sheet music. Have at least three hymns ready for a moment's notice.

22 • The MTC doesn't serve breakfast on Sunday mornings. Either plan ahead and eat a lot on Saturday night, or save something from your "care" packages.

23 · Make sure your haircut is short enough to get you through the entire MTC experience. MTC barbers don't use scissors – they only have razors!

24 • Realize that it's normal to not get any sleep the night before you enter the MTC, the first night in the MTC, and the night before you come home.

25 • Don't joke with airport security. They can and will detain you.

26 • Your president's first impression of you could last your entire mission. So look sharp when you walk off the plane to greet him.

27 • When you actually arrive in the mission field, don't panic. Even the best-prepared missionaries take a few days to adjust.

28 • Take a durable, inexpensive watch.

29 • Sing "If You Could Hie to Kolob" in district meetings.

30 • Try every "local" food at least once.

31 • Excavate the dirt out of the grooves of your name tag on a regular basis.

32 • Stargaze out the holes in your apartment ceiling.

33 • Take photos of the common, everyday scenes from each area (laundromat, supermarket, apartment).

34 • Stand every time you greet the mission president's wife.

35 ◆ Get to church early on Sundays.

36 ◆ Sing a hymn after companion study.

37 ◆ Have a picture of the Savior, the prophet, and a temple on your apartment walls.

38 ◆ Invite companions, converts, and others to write short notes in your journal.

39 ◆ Always eat a good breakfast.

40 · When your companion gets transferred, make sure you claim the apartment's best mattress and blankets.

41 ♦ Collect enough quarters for your wash *before* arriving at the laundromat.

42 ♦ Get the home address of each companion and your mission president(s). They'll expect to receive wedding invitations.

43 ♦ The Lord blesses the families of missionaries.

44 ♦ Upon arriving in a new area, find a good bakery.

45 ◆ Read to and talk with all children—in homes, on the street, and at church.

46 ◆ Find an answer for Revelation 22:18-19.

47 ◆ Learn what annoys your companion—and do it on occasion.

48 ◆ Learn what pleases your companion—and do it on occasion.

49 ◆ Cook bacon weekly, just for the smell of it.

50 • Remember to fill the font for baptisms.

51 • Take a copy of an old talk to sacrament meetings; if the bishop calls on you without warning, you'll be prepared.

52 • Get to know the missionary couples well.

53 • Read the Book of Mormon *every* day of your mission.

54 ◆ Arrange your schedule so you can tract at least a little each day.

55 ◆ Write a letter to your companion's parents, grandparents, or family.

56 ◆ When riding bikes along the street, stay in single file. It's nice to ride side by side to talk, but it invites accidents and annoys drivers.

57 • Eat frozen vegetables instead of canned vegetables.

58 • Put fun stickers on the back of your name tag—children love that.

59 • Make sure you and your companion each carry a set of keys for the apartment and car.

60 • Prepare a 2 1/2 minute talk on Mosiah 15:1-4.

61 ♦ Remember, the harder you work on your mission, the better looking your spouse will be.

62 ♦ Sing hymns while you tract, and try to harmonize.

63 ♦ Carry a pen.

64 ♦ Elders, save one new white shirt for the halfway point of your mission.

65 • Leave at least a quarter tank of gas in the car at transfer time.

66 • Create trivia questions from Church videos.

67 • Record the most creative rejections you receive in a separate section of your journal.

68 • Surprise your companion by rearranging the furniture in the apartment while he/she is in the shower.

69 • Wear thermal garments for baptisms performed outside in the winter.

70 • Don't be afraid to get your suit dirty.

71 • Store some water in 2-liter bottles in your apartment for emergencies.

72 · Don't eat food that's been in the fridge longer than you've been in the area.

73 ♦ Create two or three inside jokes
    per companionship.

74 ♦ Make treats for district meetings.

75 ♦ Write in your journal every day, preferably
    at night.

76 ♦ Draw pictures on your letters to the
    mission president.

77 ◆ Read all the standard works at least once during your mission.

78 ◆ Make bookmarks for investigators by writing a favorite scripture, thought, or hymn on a card.

79 ◆ Get a good night's rest.

80 ◆ Don't be afraid to say "I don't know."

81 • Find something to do on P-day that's not basketball.

82 • Ask yourself, "Would I be embarrassed if my mom suddenly arrived at my apartment and needed to use my bathroom?"

83 • Before visiting a hair salon in a new area, sisters should check with members to see if the shop is a reputable place.

84 ◆ Don't chew gum while tracting.

85 ◆ Laugh.

86 ◆ Cry.

87 ◆ Smile.

88 ◆ Do five push-ups a day.

89 ◆ Be obedient; but if you slip, forgive yourself–then do better next time.

90 · When a big dog chases you, remember you only have to outrun your companion, not the dog.

91 • Wear some wild socks during the Christmas season.

92 • Don't let your neck get sunburned on P-day. You'll be wearing a tie in a few hours.

93 • Buy a state/national flag from your mission.

94 ✦ Make a copy of your favorite poem or *Ensign* article for an investigator or member, just to tell him/her thanks.

95 ✦ Find one vegetable you like – and eat it occasionally.

96 ✦ Make mission Christmases your best ever.

97 ✦ Study your patriarchal blessing often.

98 • Have district/zone breakfasts on P-day.

99 • For at least one day each week, refrain from thinking about home.

100 • Encourage young people to serve missions.

101 • Encourage older couples to serve missions.

102 • Pay your bills promptly.

103 • Using natural foods and food coloring, create a green meal for your "greenie"– green salad, vegetables, rolls, drink, etc.

104 • When you have one year left, serve like you have only one month left. When you have one month left, live it like you still have a year.

105 • Tell office elders they were less valiant in the premortal world.

106 ♦ Never refuse a dinner appointment.

107 ♦ A new red sweatshirt shouldn't be washed with white shirts.

108 ♦ Put a sign on the inside of your front door, reminding you to pray every time you leave your apartment.

109 ♦ Let your junior companion be senior once in a while for practice.

110 • Drive with your windows up at night.

111 • Call your DL if you're going to be late getting home.

112 • There are few problems a hot shower and a hot meal can't solve.

113 • Read Nephi's Psalm in 2 Nephi 4:15-35.

114 • Challenge your companion to a "righteous" day—see if the two of you can keep both the letter and spirit of every mission rule.

115 • Check pockets before washing.

116 • Tell converts to bring a change of underwear for baptisms, and remember to bring a change of garments for yourself if you're performing the baptism.

117 · Write your family weekly, not weakly.

118 • Return calls to your mission president immediately.

119 • It's OK for elders to use an iron once in a while.

120 • Have new members write a letter to your family.

121 • Pray together with your companion.

122 ◆ Play "Name That Tune" with church hymns in district meetings.

123 ◆ Make dinner for an investigator using foods and recipes from home.

124 ◆ Maintain your bike.

125 ◆ It's inappropriate to count-down the hours until you'll be home (depressing, too).

126 • Make use of every rest room opportunity. You never know when you'll find another one.

127 • Drinking out of the same glass or bottle as your companion is a quick way to share illnesses.

128 • Live the law of consecration with your companion in relation to goodies from home.

129 • Don't fast longer than 24 hours—even for special investigators or challenges.

130 • If you're lucky enough to have a car, show it the respect it deserves by driving properly and washing it weekly.

131 • Garments make great gifts from home for birthdays—ask for them!

132 • Don't backbite your mission president or any other missionary leaders.

133 · Develop a scripture marking system that's personal to you and not too messy.

134 • As a senior, include your companion in the planning process, especially when training.

135 • Include childhood memories in your letters to your parents.

136 • If you disagree with your companion, remember it's not who's right but what's right.

137 ♦ Make sure there is proper ventilation for all gas appliances.

138 ♦ Send film home for developing.

139 ♦ Bring postcards from home to show investigators about your hometown.

140 ♦ Carry consecrated oil (this includes sister missionaries).

141 ♦ Sing the hymns at church.

142 • When asked what your name tag represents, tell the person it is a reminder that you are to give him/her a copy of the Book of Mormon.

143 • Sneak into another companionship's apartment while they're out and clean it.

144 • Cross-reference your patriarchal blessing to the scriptures.

145 · Send thank-you notes after dinner appointments.

146 ✦ Stretch before playing sports on P-day—
it's been seven days since you
really exercised.

147 ✦ Make sure the spare tire set in your car is
in working order.

148 ✦ Wear your seat belts.

149 ✦ Be a courteous driver.

150 • Leave notes with scriptural references on them at investigators' homes.

151 • Since P-day is short, don't spend more time in the grocery store than you have to. Make a list before you go.

152 • Buy toilet paper in bulk.

153 • Bring a Nerf football.

154 ✦ Send cards to family members on their birthdays. It takes just a little effort, but it really thrills them.

155 ✦ Leave for appointments five minutes before you think you should.

156 ✦ Take a copy of the Book of Mormon with you everywhere, even on P-day.

157 • Soften the blow from a bad day.
Buy a milk shake.

158 • The missionary who is generally last to
arrive for basketball on P-days should not
be the guardian of the sports equipment.

159 • If you serve in a foreign country, bring a
small map that you can use to show
investigators where you live.

160 · Start a false rumor
about transfers.

161 · Swap ties at zone meetings.

162 · Offer to help with the dishes at dinner appointments.

163 · Pay your fast offerings.

164 · Play hymns on your investigator's piano.

165 · Use different routes to get to the same location.

166 · Send a romantic-looking envelope addressed to yourself through the office mail system. See what rumors start surfacing.

167 · Buy postcards from each area you serve in.

168 · Remember: One golden investigator is worth 100 door slams.

169 · Make each companion
feel like he or she is
your best one yet.

170 ◆ Floss.

171 ◆ On some days, combine the lunch and dinner hours. This gives you a two-hour break in the afternoon–enough time to actually make a decent meal.

172 ◆ Don't have a specific approach in mind when a person answers the door. Be spontaneous.

173 ◆ Drink hot chocolate on cold nights.

174 ♦ Refrain from checking for mail more than twice a day.

175 ♦ Ask your parents not to send you Christmas gifts. Instead, suggest that they use the money to send gifts to your investigators and new converts.

176 ♦ Know three appropriate jokes you can share with members and investigators.

177 ♦ Eat a piece of fruit each day.

178 • Place church books in local libraries. If church books are already in the library, make sure a current local mission phone number is written on the inside front cover.

179 • Always lock your car or bike, even if you'll be away for only a minute.

180 ◆ Create a "circuit letter" with friends serving missions. Done properly, you can keep in touch with several friends but only write one letter.

181 ◆ Defrost the fridge.

182 ◆ Think twice before lending money to others…including companions.

183 ◆ Remember, your mission president is human, too.

184 ♦ Keep jewelry to a minimum. Wearing fancy jewelry is asking for a mugging.

185 ♦ With your companion, select a key word for the day that must be worked into door approaches.

186 ♦ Avoid wearing sunglasses. People like to see your eyes.

187 ♦ Always try "one more door."

188 • If it's OK with the bishop, greet the members of the ward as they arrive at church.

189 • Wash the dishes before going to bed.

190 • Start each discussion by talking about what you personally read in the Book of Mormon that morning.

191 • Send baptismal forms to the office immediately.

192 • Base your cold cereal purchasing decision on the prize offered in the box.

193 • Be punctual for everything.

194 • Create an exercise program that results in a cleaner apartment (for example, waxing the floor).

195 · Never refer to a baptism as anything other than a baptism (such as a "dunking").

196 • Carve a jack-o'-lantern out of a watermelon.

197 • When in doubt, tract.

198 • Wake your companion one morning with a flash picture.

199 • Obey the speed limit.

200 • Stay within your allotted mileage.

201 · Don't sweep dirt under the rug…unless the mission president and his wife just drove up.

202 · Drink orange juice.

203 · Make sure "companion splits" are quality time, not goof-off time, especially when your "companion du jour" is a member rather than a full-time missionary.

204 • Write some poetry.

205 • Don't teach a wife or a child without first meeting the man of the house and explaining what you want to do.

206 • A tidy apartment invites the Spirit.

207 • Regularly tell your companion that you love him/her – and why.

208 · When traveling to an area to tract, don't be in such a hurry that you overlook the hundreds of people you pass along the way.

209 • Don't leave dirty dishes when you're transferred.

210 • Know the mission song by heart and sing it enthusiastically. If your mission doesn't have a song, write one.

211 • Always have some money on hand.

212 • Don't do a door approach with your hands in your pockets.

213 • Write riddles and puzzles on letters to your mission president, but don't include the answers until next week.

214 • Be consistent. If you teach one thing and do another, your message becomes void.

215 • Create a zone Christmas card to be sent to the other missionaries in your mission.

216 • Be patient.

217 • Carry a toy with you. Pull it out when young children start disrupting a discussion.

218 • Always greet the bishop at church at your first opportunity.

219 • Write to prospective missionaries in your home ward.

220 • Put Heinz 57 sauce on top of all meals you cook to kill the "missionary" taste.

221 • Discuss the upcoming appointment with your companion while commuting to it.

222 • Create new words to Primary songs.

223 • Lock your apartment door whenever you leave and before going to bed. Leave a light on when you're out at night.

224 • Don't linger after dinner appointments.

225 ◆ Carry a photo of your family in
your wallet.

226 ◆ Stay awake while your companion drives.

227 ◆ Drink eight glasses of water a day.

228 ◆ Your journal should be a record of both
your activities and your thoughts.

229 • If your alarm clock breaks, buy a new one. Don't use it as an excuse for not getting up on time.

230 • Have a pillow fight with your companion.

231 • Attend Bible study classes and be a friendly participant.

232 · How you act on P-day is
a direct reflection of how
you will act when you are
a returned missionary.

233 • In letters to your parents, thank them for doing specific things during your childhood, such as teaching you correct principles, giving you good examples, etc.

234 • Get plants for your apartment.

235 • Have food on hand for Sundays in case your dinner appointment cancels. Don't be in a situation where you feel compelled to go to the store on the Sabbath.

236 • On hot days, take a cold shower during your lunch break.

237 • Read one chapter from Proverbs a day. In one month, you'll have read them all.

238 • Leave a list of free P-day activities in your area book.

239 • Tell your companion "good night" every night.

240 • After holding a district or zone meeting at the chapel, leave the building in the same condition you found it.

241 • Occasionally write an individualized letter to one family member instead of to the whole family.

242 • Surprise your landlord with a small gift.

243 • Say meal prayers with your companion.

244 • Look forward to your interview with the mission president. Have a question in mind to ask him.

245 • Talk with the members, not at them.

246 • Be a considerate tenant in your apartment building.

247 • Remember, suits can be taken to dry cleaners. Take them in at least once a year.

248 • Wash hands after using the bathroom.

249 • Wipe toothpaste out of the sink.

250 • Learn from your mistakes and don't make the same one twice.

251 • Don't aspire to leadership. Once you get it, you'll regret it.

252 • Get up early once in a while and make breakfast for your companion.

253 · Service projects at rest homes are very rewarding.

254 · Remember the concept of "mail lag." If you ask your parents for advice about something minor, the problem will probably be resolved before they can respond.

255 · When answering the phone in your apartment, use your name.

256 • Use stain spray on the collars of white shirts/blouses.

257 • Don't wash the dishes while your companion is in the shower. Missionary apartments generally have pretty low water pressure in the first place.

258 • Shake hands with all people.

259 · Be able to tell one
Book of Mormon story
dynamically by memory.

260 ◆ Figure out a budget for the month and then try to spend at least $10 less than that.

261 ◆ Don't make fun of local dialects.

262 ◆ Keep fast offering receipts in the envelope with your patriarchal blessing and mission call. That way, you'll always know where they are.

263 ◆ Don't confess or discuss past sins with investigators or members.

264 ◆ Get a haircut the first P-day of each month.

265 ◆ Leave enough time to fill the font for baptisms, and make sure you or someone who will be at the baptism knows how to turn on the water for the font, including the hot water.

266 ◆ Find little ways to give community service.

267 ◆ Compile a "ratings guide" for all of the apartments in the mission and mail a copy to the APs.

268 ◆ Check with parents before promising members or investigators free room and board when they visit you back home.

269 ♦ Once in a while, call your companion by his/her first name and see if he/she responds.

270 ♦ There's no such thing as "P-day Eve."

271 ♦ Answer the questions your mother asks in her letters.

272 ♦ Find out if your apartment has a garbage disposal before putting food down the sink.

273 • Don't visit members only at the time when your favorite TV show comes on.

274 • Clothes dry faster if you clean the lint out of the dryer first.

275 • Assign your companion the hard questions.

276 • Don't write your girlfriend/boyfriend every day—she/he may end up marrying the mail carrier.

277 · Make sure your parents save your letters home. This acts as a back-up journal in case something happens to the one you have in the mission field.

278 · Have a district meeting that focuses on bike and car safety.

279 · Before entering a yard, shake the gate to check for dogs.

280 • Your journal is being written for posterity. Use a pen instead of a pencil.

281 • When teaching a first discussion, use the new investigator's Bible instead of yours. Though the wording may be slightly different, it allows the person to see that the verses you share are in his/her version.

282 • Tuck your pant leg into your sock before riding your bike.

283 · Be especially nice to the mission president the week before transfers.

284 • Early on in the discussions, set up a fellowshipper for your investigator.

285 • Don't visit church members on Monday evenings unless you have been invited by them to do so.

286 • When your investigator leaves the room for a few minutes, swap ties with your companion and see if he/she notices.

287 ♦ Trust your mission president. He is entitled to inspiration on your behalf.

288 ♦ If you have an answering machine, make sure the message is tasteful and appropriate.

289 ♦ Don't solicit dinner appointments.

290 ♦ When training, carefully plan your new companion's first night so it includes a combination of tracting and teaching.

291 • Tracting in a threesome isn't a good idea. It looks like the Mafia has arrived on the doorstep.

292 • Don't let non-missionaries ride in mission cars.

293 • Play miniature golf at least once a month on P-day.

294 • When a customs officer asks you if you have anything to declare, respond with, "Yes, we are living in an era when the gospel has been restored."

295 • Label your photos immediately with full names.

296 • Don't refer to missionaries as "studs."

297 ♦ Avoid purple ties.

298 ♦ Remember the missionary version of D&C 4:3: "If ye have desires to serve God [in a particular area of your mission], ye are called to the work [in the opposite end of the mission]."

299 ♦ Never insult the owner of a pit bull.

300 ♦ Live your mission with no regrets.

301 • Along with your regular stats on the letter to the president, include fun stats such as how many times you had a door slammed in your face, how many times your companion annoyed you, and what your basketball shooting percentage was on P-day.

302 • Go out to eat on hump day.

303 ◆ After removing your socks at night, safety pin them together. It saves you from sorting socks after doing your laundry.

304 ◆ Helaman 10:5 says you will be blessed even after your mission if you give it your all while you're out there.

305 ◆ Keep aspirin, Tylenol, or ibuprofen on hand.

306 ◆ Don't be alone with the opposite sex.

307 ◆ Create "Mormon cigarettes"—rolled-up pieces of paper with scriptures on them—for investigators who smoke.

308 ◆ Alma 8:19 is a great "dinner appointment" scripture.

309 ◆ If you hang shirts immediately after coming out of the dryer, ironing can be greatly reduced.

310 ◆ Limit candy bar consumption to one a day.

311 ◆ If you shower first, don't use all the hot water.

312 ◆ Learn to forgive. You'll have lots of opportunities.

313 ◆ Spend half of one district meeting allowing missionaries to write in their journals.

314 • It's difficult to diet if only half the companionship is participating.

315 • If you bear your testimony in sacrament meeting, keep it short, simple, and basic. This meeting is for the members. You can bear your testimony at the next zone or district meeting.

316 ⋅ Members won't be transferred on Thursday, but you might be. Make sure investigators get attached to members rather than you.

317 • Sisters should take one nice dress for baptismal services and other important occasions. Other outfits should be durable, but still nice looking.

318 • Occasionally make your companion's bed.

319 • Don't be afraid to make a fool of yourself when learning the language.

320 • Photocopy one letter and send it to several people.

321 • Have members sit with investigators at church.

322 • If you receive several letters one day, don't open all of them that day. You might not get any tomorrow.

323 • Get to know the members in your ward who are good at repairing bikes.

324 · Arrange to have members invite investigators over for family home evening.

325 · During the time you are called to be a missionary, you are entitled to special insights into the scriptures. As you receive them, write them in the margins of your scriptures so you'll remember them when you come home.

326 • Having companion study leads to a good day.

327 • Find the good qualities in all people.

328 • Save baptismal programs for your scrapbook.

329 • One of the best ways to learn the language is to read the Book of Mormon *out loud* in the language of your mission.

330 • If you have an electric shaver, clear the whiskers out of it periodically.

331 • Keep popcorn on hand.

332 • You don't actually have to throw rocks at dogs to scare them. Just picking up a rock, or acting like you're picking up a rock, will generally scare them.

333 • After accomplishing one goal, move on to another.

334 • Most sisters can get by with minimal makeup.

335 • Don't try to "endure" a companionship, figuring you'll be transferred soon. Most mission presidents keep companions together until they can work through the problems and learn to love each other.

336 · When you're a "greenie," you may think your trainer is the worst missionary in the Church. Be sure you write and thank him/her a few months later when you realize how good he/she was.

337 · Don't feel guilty doing something fun on P-day.

338 · It's best to buy most of your souvenirs at the end of your mission.

339 · If you don't approach the
stranger on the street,
the answer is already no.

340 • Take flea powder if you're sent to South America.

341 • Review goals often.

342 • Let your senior companion do his/her job.

343 • Clean the toilet weekly.

344 • Keep a list of less-active members and visit several each week.

345 ◆ Follow your mission president's counsel, even if it doesn't make any sense to you at the time.

346 ◆ On the last page of your copy of the Book of Mormon, record the dates that you finish reading it. This will help you keep track of the number of times you read it during your mission.

347 • When learning a foreign language, carry a notebook to write down new words you learn.

348 • Sisters shouldn't laugh at elders when they say their girlfriend is waiting for them.

349 • Even after triple locking your bike, don't be surprised when it's stolen.

350 • Before complaining about companionship problems to other missionaries, talk to your companion.

351 • Sweats are great for a mission. Besides being great for P-day, they are perfect for sleeping.

352 • At the end of the day, identify one miracle that occurred.

353 • Suggest that the investigator be baptized by a local member and not by one of the missionary elders.

354 • If you're not happy, work harder.

355 • Don't cross off days on your calendar.

356 • Buy a squirt gun with your companion for apartment duels.

357 ♦ Let investigators make the decision for baptism.

358 ♦ Don't be too hard on yourself and become depressed. That's what Satan wants.

359 ♦ Obey all customs and visa regulations.

360 ♦ When writing your parents, remember they like to know the nitty-gritty basic stuff.

361 • Enjoy your companion while you can. A few days after transfers, you'll probably want him/her back.

362 • You should still get up on time on P-day. But it's OK to take a nap shortly after you get up!

363 • Send your mom a Mother's Day card–in
September.

364 • When conducting a baptismal interview,
ask the baptismal candidate to say the
opening prayer.

365 • After the first discussion, ask the family if
you can kneel down together for the
closing prayer.

366 • Record the best missionary folklore stories you hear in your journal. Some examples include disobedient missionaries being spotted at major sporting events and the Three Nephites coming to the aid of a companionship.

367 • See if you can create a new missionary folklore story.

368 ◆ For sisters, low-heeled shoes are more convenient and comfortable than high heels.

369 ◆ Always read a scripture before leaving a member's house. Mosiah 2:41 is a good one to use.

370 ◆ Believe your beliefs and doubt your doubts.

371 · Be honest in your letters
to your parents.

372 ◆ Never criticize another church or denomination.

373 ◆ Emphasize the elements of the right side of the discussion booklets. Though the left side contains the actual doctrine, the right side includes the elements that bring in the Spirit.

374 ◆ Elders and sisters should keep their relationship on a professional level at all times.

375 • Create a visual Plan of Salvation chart for the fourth discussion. If you have a layout from the premortal life to the three degrees of glory, your investigators will understand it more easily.

376 • Hold an ugly tie contest.

377 • Pick one General Conference address every two weeks and study it thoroughly.

378 · Never, ever haze or initiate new missionaries. The missionary force is a brotherhood and sister-hood, not a fraternity or sorority.

379 • Don't be afraid to say a prayer when visiting a less-active member.

380 • Whenever you obey the advice given by the mission president's wife at zone conference, great blessings will follow.

381 • During personal study time, share your insights with your companion.

382 • Remember, even on P-days people know you're a missionary. Don't embarrass yourself, your parents, the mission, or the Church in your choice of activities.

383 • Don't call home – ever. Besides being against Church policy, calling home makes you depressed for at least 30 minutes after the call.

384 • When time rolls around for mission skits, use Church videos as the premise, but change the plot.

385 • Try to visit everyone on the branch or ward list, even though you may be told that certain families "aren't worth the effort."

386 ◆ Your sewing kit should be heavy on black and white thread and light on colored thread.

387 ◆ Inform your parents that packages sent from an airport mail office arrive at least a day sooner than those sent at the neighborhood post office.

388 • Let your companion teach part of the discussion, no matter how inept he or she seems with the language or the discussions.

389 • Humor should never degrade.

390 • Don't spend all of P-day writing letters. You'll see your friends and family again, but you may never see this part of the world again.

391 • Make sure you write legibly enough in your journal and in letters home that a Urim and Thummim will not be needed to translate.

392 • Don't assume the church building will be available on the date and time you have chosen for a baptismal service. Always double check.

393 ✦ Act on all impressions to do good.

394 ✦ Always add to your finding pool, even if your teaching and baptizing pools are high. It's amazing how quickly you can find yourself with no investigators.

395 ✦ When a missionary receives a "Dear John," don't brag that the same thing will never happen to you.

396 ♦ Don't leave valuables in clear view inside your car. Place them in the trunk.

397 ♦ Establish a reputation for doing something outstanding, like having immaculately shined shoes, sharply pressed trousers, or a missionary haircut.

398 · Respect missionaries from other religions. Like you, they believe they have been called to do a work among God's children.

399 • Need a diversionary tactic to minimize the practice time at district and zone meetings? Ask a lot of questions!

400 • When you're having difficulties with a companion, realize that God loves him/her as much as He loves and cares for you.

401 • During discussions, bear testimony of what your companion has just taught.

402 • Don't take yourself too seriously.

403 • Be the type of missionary your parents think you are.

404 • Spend a week studying 2 Nephi 9.

405 • Remember names, not numbers.

406 • Resist the urge to read or view anti-Mormon material. Some missionaries may say it will help you be a better missionary, but all it does is fill your mind with false doctrines and uncertainty.

407 • Try to have your investigators talk about 50 percent of the time when you teach a discussion.

408 • To get through companion study faster, play the Missionary Guide tapes on high speed.

409 • When you and your companion are asked to speak in a meeting, do the generous thing: speak for one minute and leave the rest of the time for your companion.

410 • Don't create problems for the next set of missionaries who will move into your area.

411 • When you have 138 days left, begin reading the Doctrine & Covenants from the back—one section a day.

412 • On your final Valentine's Day in the mission field, realize that next year's Valentine's Day will probably be just as lonely.

413 • Give away some of your clothing to members and missionaries before leaving to come home.

414 • Remember the principles of the commitment pattern when you return home and start dating.

415 ♦ Give out at least one Book of Mormon on the flight home.

416 ♦ You aren't released until you've visited with your stake president. So if you travel after your mission, remember to still follow missionary rules.

417 • Wear your most worn-out suit for your home-coming instead of new clothes. This will make it look like you worked really hard.

418 ♦ Write a letter to your future children as soon as you get home, summarizing your mission and what you learned. Plan to give it to them just before they enter the mission field.

419 ♦ Avoid travelogues in your homecoming address.

420 ◆ No one knows what you're saying when you bear your testimony in your mission's language at your homecoming – unless you went to an English-speaking mission.

421 ◆ To say your mission was the best two years of your life is a bit inaccurate. It's OK to say it was the toughest, most challenging, yet most rewarding two years of your life.

422 ◆ Read this book only on P-day.